LOUISA LEARNS TO WRITE

Louisa May Alcott Creates *Little Women*

KATE HANNIGAN

Illustrated by
SOFIA MOORE

CALKINS CREEK

AN IMPRINT OF ASTRA BOOKS FOR YOUNG READERS
New York

"I like good strong words that mean something."

—Jo March in *Little Women*

When the three Alcott sisters were born in the 1830s, Louisa was tucked in the middle between Anna and Elizabeth. And right there—at the heart of the family—was where she stayed her whole life.

~READ~

Father was a teacher and always changing jobs. After a fourth daughter arrived, the family often had only bread and apples to eat and hand-me-down clothes to wear. What they lacked in riches, Anna, Louisa, Lizzie, and baby May made up for in the colorful worlds they found in the pages of books.

"One of my earliest recollections is of playing with books in my father's study—building houses and bridges of the big dictionaries and diaries . . ."

~WRITE~

Louisa loved to climb trees and run through the woods, sometimes under moonlight. On her tenth birthday, Mother presented her with a special gift. Opening the pages of a journal, Louisa let the words flow—from poetry to petty complaints and even private dreams.

"I give you the pencil-case I promised,
for I have observed that you are fond of writing,
and wish to encourage the habit."

—Louisa's mother, Abby May Alcott,
November 1842

"I wrote in my Imagination Book,
and enjoyed it very much.
Life is pleasanter than it used to be."

~OBSERVE~

The Alcotts moved from house to house, barely scraping by to earn a living. Eldest sisters Anna and Louisa worked too, first doing chores at home, then later as teachers, seamstresses, governesses, and domestic servants.

Louisa noticed their hands were more calloused and their gowns more faded than those of other girls their age.

"I wish I was rich,
I was good, and we were all
a happy family this day."

~PLAY~

"In those days a red scarf, a long cloak, a big hat with a plume stolen from a bonnet, a paper-knife dagger . . . tissue paper stretched on wire hoops for fairy wings, produced superb effects."

—Edward Emerson, Louisa's friend

When Louisa was twelve, Mother's inheritance helped them buy a new home they called Hillside in Concord, Massachusetts. With a room of her own, Louisa was finally able to lose herself in reading, writing, and dreaming. Here the "golden band of sisters," as Father called them, had fun sewing costumes, building sets, and bringing Louisa's stories to life.

Walking the woods with her neighbor, the philosopher Henry David Thoreau, Louisa explored new places and new ways of thinking. On family visits to friends like the writers Nathaniel Hawthorne and Ralph Waldo Emerson, the Alcotts discussed issues like education, the role of women, and slavery.

~EXPLORE~

The family put their beliefs into action, making Hillside a stop on the Underground Railroad, a network of safe houses that sheltered men and women escaping slavery.

~DReaM~

Bills piled up, so the Alcotts moved to Boston in search of jobs. After long days mending clothes and tending to children, Louisa picked up her pen and imagined herself a professional writer. She dreamed of buying dresses for her sisters, an easy chair for Mother, warm slippers for Father, and a cozy house where they'd live together.

"I will do something by and by.
Don't care what, teach, sew, act, write,
anything to help the family; and I'll be rich and
famous and happy before I die, see if I won't!"

After moving over a dozen times, they finally found a
cheerful new home called Orchard House. But to Louisa's
great sorrow, the band of sisters was breaking apart.
Lizzie had caught scarlet fever in 1856 and never
fully recovered. After two years, she passed away.
Not long after, Anna fell in love and married,
leaving home to start a new family.

"[N]ow that death and love have taken
two of us away, I can, I hope, soon manage
to care for the remaining four."

~FAIL~

Louisa threw her energy into writing for newspapers, magazines, even book publishers—sometimes under a fictitious name or anonymously. She wrote late at night and in stolen hours throughout the day, her pen flowing with "blood and thunder" thrillers, melodramas, and fanciful fairy tales. Money and praise trickled in, but not everyone was positive. One editor told her,

"Stick to your teaching, Miss Alcott. You can't write."

~EXPERIMENT~

Louisa didn't lose hope. And she didn't stop writing, even when the Civil War broke out and she stepped up to help. Serving as a nurse in the nation's capital, she wrote letters describing the wounded and dying. Once she was back home, Louisa turned those letters into a novel, this time trying a straightforward, realistic style. *Hospital Sketches* became a hit with readers and critics.

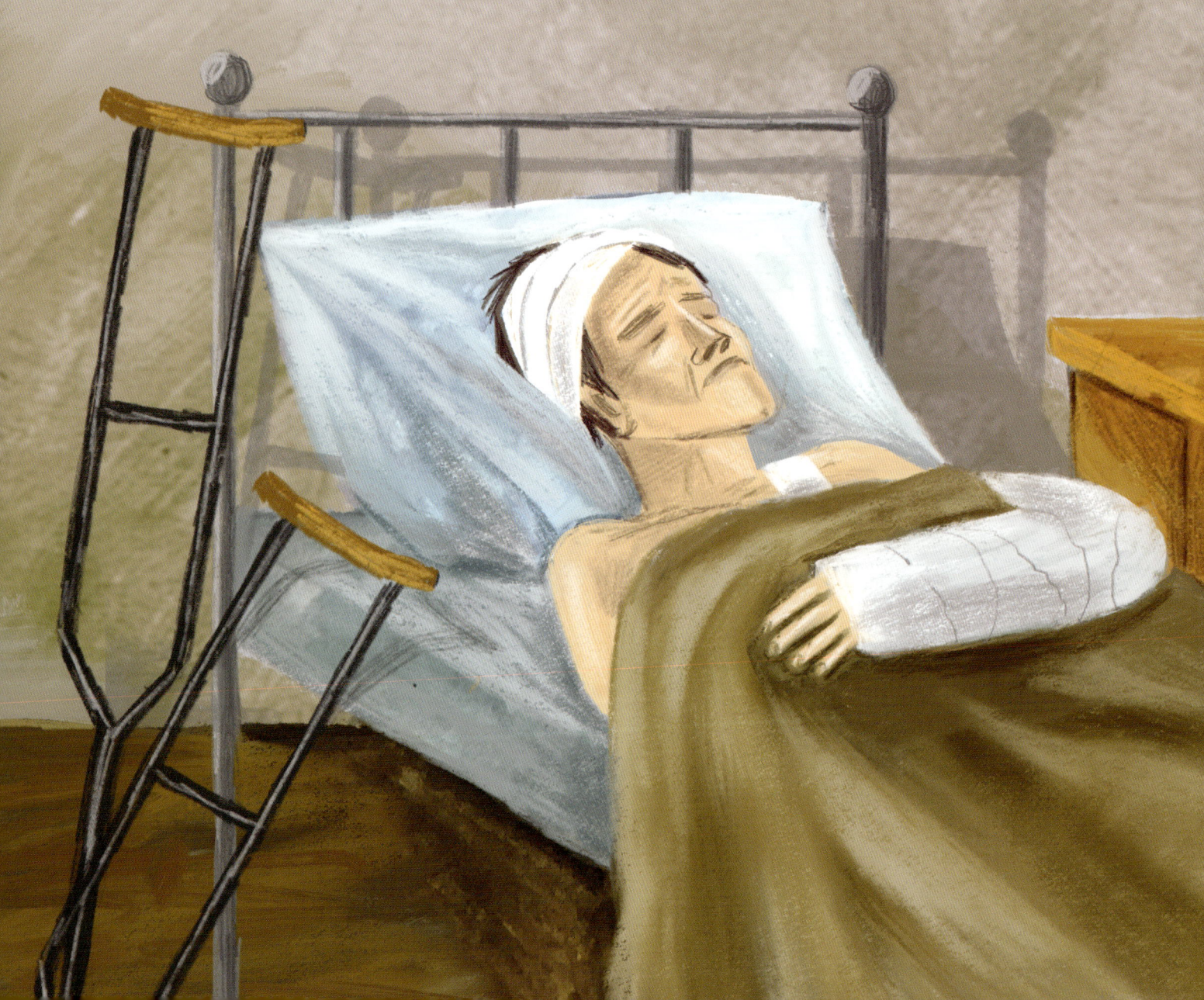

"I can write,
    and I'll prove it."

~PERSEVERE~

She kept writing, dipping her pen into the inkwell and filling page after page. When her right hand ached, she switched to the left.

"The fit was on strong, and for a fortnight I hardly ate, slept, or stirred, but wrote, wrote, like a thinking machine in full operation."

Louisa was starting to earn enough to pay off her family's debts when a publisher made a special request. There were lots of popular books written for boys. Would she write one for girls?

"[L]ively, simple books are very much needed for girls, and perhaps I can supply the need."

~DARE~

Louisa turned to the girls she knew best—her sisters.
Anna, Lizzie, and May inspired the characters Meg,
Beth, and Amy March. And "Lu," as her family called
her, became Jo.

Over ten quick weeks, she wrote from her heart, tapping the skills she'd developed and all she remembered of growing up. Especially how it felt to be a girl with big dreams.

Louisa called it *Little Women.*

"It reads better than I expected . . .
we really lived most of it, and if it succeeds,
that will be the reason of it."

Author's Note

Released in two parts in 1868 and 1869, Louisa May Alcott's *Little Women* was an immediate best seller, with readers snapping it up as quickly as her publisher could print copies. Since then, it's been translated into dozens of languages and has never gone out of print in over 150 years. It's been adapted into movies and plays set in different eras and cultures and loved by everyone from President Theodore Roosevelt to Supreme Court Justice Ruth Bader Ginsburg.

Generations of readers have drawn inspiration from the strong, independent March sisters—especially rebellious Jo. Being as smart as any boy and just as fast, both Jo and Louisa believed girls, like boys, should have opportunities to make a decent living: "I want to do something splendid," Jo says, ". . . something heroic or wonderful that won't be forgotten after I'm dead . . . . I think I shall write books, and get rich and famous; that would suit me, so that is my favorite dream."

Louisa went on to write many more books, and her name has not been forgotten. Nor have her characters. While she couldn't keep her "golden band of sisters" together in real life, she could make Anna, Lizzie, and May live forever on the page.

Touching on universal themes of love, grief, struggle, and independence, *Little Women* was one of the first books to shine a light on the lives of ordinary girls—flaws and all. It's inspired countless women to become writers and remains a treasured exploration of childhood, sisterhood, and growing up.

Louisa May Alcott, 1858 daguerreotype

Anna Alcott, 1858 daguerreotype

Elizabeth "Lizzie" Alcott, 1855 crayon sketch by Caroline Hildreth

May Alcott, 1877 oil painting by Rosa Peckham

Ten Habits for Becoming a Writer

READ
Pick up a book and get lost in a story.

WRITE
The more we put pencil to paper,
the easier writing becomes.

OBSERVE
Use all five senses to notice details
both large and small.

PLAY
World-building is a form of storytelling.

EXPLORE
Discover different kinds of books and ideas.

DREAM
Quiet time frees our imagination.

FAIL
Don't be afraid to see what works—
and what does not.

EXPERIMENT
Try different styles of writing.

PERSEVERE
Keep at it, even when things get tough.

DARE
Find the courage to reach a little bit higher.

Louisa May Alcott Timeline

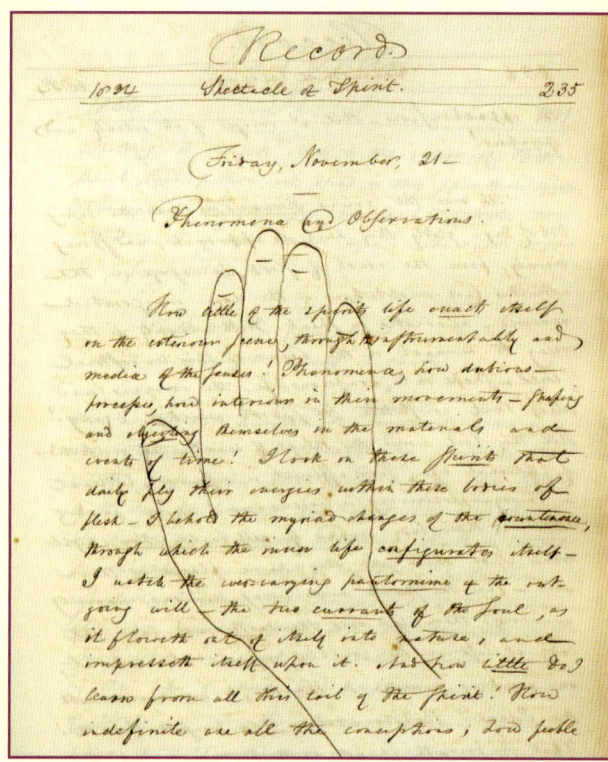

Everyone in the Alcott family was encouraged to write in a daily journal, and Louisa started at an early age. In this page from one of her father Bronson Alcott's journals, he has drawn an outline of two-year-old Louisa's hand.

1831 March 16
Big sister Anna Bronson Alcott is born to Bronson Alcott, an educator and philosopher, and Abby May Alcott, a social worker, in Philadelphia's Germantown community.

1832 November 29
Louisa May Alcott is born.

1835 June 24
Elizabeth "Lizzie" Alcott is born.

1840 July 26
Abigail May Alcott is born.

1843 June
Moves with family to Fruitlands, a utopian farming commune founded by her father and his friends outside Boston, Massachusetts, where members use no animal labor nor animal products, follow a diet of mostly water and fruit, and reject cotton fabric because its production used labor from enslaved people.

1845 April 1
Moves to Hillside in Concord after mother inherits money.

1846 March
Is given her own room; Hillside becomes foundation for *Little Women*.

1849–1851
Moves with family to Boston, writes articles and stories, publishes poem under pen name "Flora Fairfield."

1854 December 9
Publishes her first book, *Flower Fables*, a collection of stories she invented for her young neighbor Ellen Emerson, Ralph Waldo Emerson's daughter.

1857
After multiple moves, family acquires Orchard House, a farmhouse with apple trees in Concord; they move into the home by the next spring.

"Miss Louisa M. Alcott will win great praise from young and old for the sweet, natural story, told with so much spirit, of *Little Women*."

—*Boston Daily Advertiser*, October 10, 1868

1858 March 14

Lizzie dies at age 22 after contracting scarlet fever; the next month Anna announces her engagement to John Pratt.

1860 May 23

Anna and John marry at Orchard House.

1862 December

Inspired by the writings of famed nurse Florence Nightingale, volunteers to serve as a Civil War nurse at a Union army hospital in Washington, DC.

1863 January

Contracts typhoid fever and becomes deathly sick; is brought back to Orchard House by her father; remains in poor health the rest of her life.

1863 August

Publishes the novel *Hospital Sketches*, a fictionalized wartime account drawn from letters she wrote during her service as a nurse.

1863–1872

Writes dozens of suspense, romance, and thriller stories with titles like *Pauline's Passion and Punishment* for magazines and newspapers, sometimes using the pen name "A. M. Barnard" and other times anonymously.

1865

Travels to Europe as a companion to a woman in ill health.

1867

Considers an editor's suggestion to write a book for girls; takes job as an editor for *Merry's Museum*, a children's magazine.

1868 May

Begins writing *Little Women*.

Writing desk Louisa's father built for her at Orchard House, where she wrote *Little Women* in 1868

1868 September 30

First volume of *Little Women* publishes followed by *Part II* the next year; the volumes are combined under the title *Little Women or Meg, Jo, Beth, and Amy*; more stories of the March family follow in *Little Men* (1871) and *Jo's Boys* (1886).

1877 November 25

Mother dies.

1879 December 29

Sister May dies a month after giving birth to a daughter she named Louisa May "Lulu" Nieriker; Louisa becomes Lulu's guardian.

1888 March 6

Dies of a stroke just two days after her father's death; her grave lies on "Author's Ridge" in Concord's Sleepy Hollow Cemetery alongside her family, as well as Thoreau, Hawthorne, and Emerson.

"Pleasant notices and letters arrive, and much interest in my little women, who seem to find friends by their truth to life, as I hoped."

—October 30, 1868

THE FACTS
in Louisa's World

THE FICTION
in *Little Women*

THE FACTS in Louisa's World	THE FICTION in *Little Women*
Mother's family name is a month: May	Family name is a month: March
Four Alcott sisters: ∿ Anna, nicknamed "Nan" ∿ Louisa, nicknamed "Lu" ∿ Elizabeth, nicknamed "Lizzie" ∿ Abigail May, nicknamed "May"	Four March sisters: ∿ Meg ∿ Jo ∿ Beth ∿ Amy (letters in "May" rearranged)
Spirited and athletic Louisa dreams of being an author.	Spirited and athletic Jo dreams of being an author.
Louisa goes running: "I always thought I must have been a deer or a horse in some former state, because it was such a joy to run."	Jo goes running: "I wish I was a horse, then I could run for miles in this splendid air, and not lose my breath."
Poor and often hungry, the sisters wear their cousins' hand-me-down dresses.	Not wealthy, but comfortable enough to employ Hannah, a cook/maid.
Times are so difficult, Louisa considers cutting her hair for money.	Mother must travel to their ailing father, so Jo cuts her hair for money.
Mother works tirelessly to support them.	Mother works tirelessly to support them.
Father unable to provide for family.	Father appears as a minor character.
Louisa serves in the Civil War as a nurse.	Father serves in the Civil War as a chaplain.
The Alcotts eat a limited diet of only vegetables that grow up, not down; they consume no animals and use no animal labor.	The Marches consume meats like turkey and chicken and treats like plum pudding, limes, cake, and ice cream.
Anna falls in love and marries.	Meg falls in love and marries.
Lizzie catches scarlet fever and dies.	Beth catches scarlet fever and dies.
May is an artist and studies in Europe.	Amy is an artist and studies in Europe.
Louisa finds happiness in "freedom and a pen."	Jo finds happiness in marriage and a family.

Bibliography

All quotations used in the book can be found in the following sources marked with an asterisk (*).

Newspapers and Magazines
*Boston Daily Advertiser. "Books of the Season." October 10, 1868.

*Emerson, Edward W. "When Louisa Alcott Was a Girl." Ladies Home Journal, December 1898.

Books
*Alcott, Louisa May. The Girlhood Diary of Louisa May Alcott, 1843–1846: Writings of a Young Author. Mankato, MN: Blue Earth Books, 2001.

*——. Little Women or Meg, Jo, Beth, and Amy. Boston: Little, Brown, and Company, 1922.

Cheever, Susan. Louisa May Alcott: A Personal Biography. New York: Simon & Schuster, 2010.

*Cheney, Ednah D., ed. Louisa May Alcott, Her Life, Letters, and Journals. Boston: Little, Brown, and Company, 1898.

Eiselein, Gregory, and Anne K. Phillips, eds. The Louisa May Alcott Encyclopedia. Westport, CT: Greenwood Press, 2001.

Myerson, Joel, Daniel Shealy, and Madeleine B. Stern, eds. The Selected Letters of Louisa May Alcott. Athens: University of Georgia Press, 1995.

*Reisen, Harriet. Louisa May Alcott: The Woman Behind "Little Women." New York: Henry Holt and Co., 2009.

Rioux, Anne Boyd. Meg, Jo, Beth, Amy: The Story of "Little Women" and Why It Still Matters. New York: W. W. Norton, 2018.

Seiple, Samantha. Louisa on the Front Lines: Louisa May Alcott in the Civil War. Cypress, California: Seal Press, 2019.

Website
Louisa May Alcott's Orchard House. louisamayalcott.org.

Acknowledgments

Grateful thanks to Zoë Hill, reference librarian at Harvard's Houghton Library, for help with images. And to scholars Gregory Eiselein and Anne K. Phillips, editors of all things Alcott, including The Louisa May Alcott Encyclopedia, for their expertise and sharp eyes. And to Jan Turnquist, executive director of Louisa May Alcott's Orchard House, for her enthusiasm and encouragement.

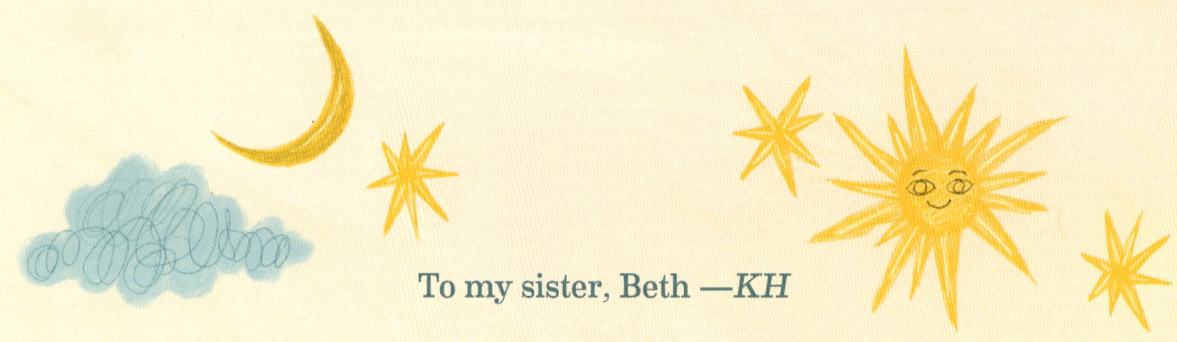

To my sister, Beth —*KH*

To my daughter, Mila May, who is a reader
and an artist who tells stories through her art —*SM*

Picture Credits

Used by permission of Louisa May Alcott's Orchard House: 34 (all), Trey Powers: 37; Printed with permission of the Houghton Library, Harvard University, MS Am 1130.10 (6): 36.

Calkins Creek
An imprint of Astra Books for Young Readers, a division of Astra Publishing House
astrapublishinghouse.com
Printed in China

ISBN: 978-1-62979-456-3 (hc)
ISBN: 978-1-63592-858-7 (eBook)
Library of Congress Control Number: 2025935722

First edition

10 9 8 7 6 5 4 3 2 1

Design by Barbara Grzeslo and Michelle Mayhall
The text is set in Avenir LT Std and Eames Century Modern.
The illustrations are done in paint, pencils, and digital.